Mufti Ras

An Early

First Draft Publishing/*Primary*

Mufti Rasheed Ludhianvi: Obedience to the Amir
An Early Text on the Afghan Taliban Movement
Semple and Mitha: Commentary and Translation

Published in Germany in 2015
by First Draft Publishing GmbH, © Mufti Rasheed

Commentary and Translation: © Michael Semple
and Yameema Mitha 2015

ISBN 978-3-944214-21-4 *(softcover)*
ISBN 978-3-944214-20-7 *(kindle)*
ISBN 978-3-944214-22-1 *(epub)*

Cover Photography: © Philip Poupin
www.philippoupin.fr
Concept & Design: Bureau Christoph Dunst
www.christophdunst.com
Typefaces: Heimat Mono *www.atlasfonts.com*
& *Arnhem www.ourtype.be*

First Draft Publishing GmbH, Berlin

www.firstdraft-publishing.com
info@firstdraft-publishing.com

Table of Contents

I. Mufti Abdul Rasheed Ludhianvi, an appraisal

1. INTRODUCTION

One day in 1934, a bearded Indian man deposited two of his sons, the younger of whom was only eleven years old, on a train in Mian Channu, Punjab,[1] which was then a part of British-ruled India. Among the passengers the father spotted a "gentleman". Imported into Urdu, the English word gentleman conveys a strong hint of disdain and irony, which could be used either for an Englishman or a westernised Indian who had adopted the mannerisms of the colonialists. The father, whose name was Maulana Mohammad Saleem, asked the gentleman to ensure that the boys got off safely in Multan. As the train steamed off across the great flood plains of Punjab, the gentleman struck up a conversation with his two charges. When he asked them the purpose of their travel, they explained that they were on their way to commence religious studies in a madrassa near Multan. Their new found chaperone was clearly not shy of expressing his opinion. He berated them over the course in life their father had chosen for them. He warned them that their time in the madrassa would be wasted and that if they finally qualified as mullahs they would be no good to anyone. The boys spoke respectfully, but did not even attempt to defend their family's attachment to traditional education, in front of this secular modernist.

Nearly seventy years after the encounter on a Punjab train, the United Nations Security Council imposed sanctions on the trust fund which one of the boys on the train had gone on to fund. By then he was known to the world as Mufti Abdul Rasheed and had become one of Pakistan's leading Sunni clerics and theorists of jihad. The Rasheed Trust stands accused of supporting Afghanistan's Taliban Movement and Al-Qaeda[2]. Far from being deterred from entering a madrassa, the son of Maulana Mohammad Saleem went on to pursue a long and distinguished career of Islamic scholarship. This involved some thirty years of study with teachers he sought out in Punjab, Sindh and Dar ul Uloom Deoband, after which he established himself as a theologian in his own right. His funeral in Karachi in 2002 attracted thousands of students and followers who had been inspired by his teachings. The institutions which he founded, including the Dar ul-Ifta o Ershad and the Rasheed Trust thrived after his demise, notwithstanding the UN sanctions.

In many ways the life and teachings of Mufti Abdul Rasheed exemplify the confrontation underlying the "war on terror". The protagonists, the apologists of violent jihad and counter-terror, imagine and represent themselves and the other in ways which the other would barely recognise. The imaginations driving this mismatched confrontation involve not just two parallel universes, but two pairs of parallel universes. It was Mufti Abdul Rasheed's role in life to idealise the world of Islam, and demonise the corrupt and cruel powers which futilely resisted the word of God. For him, this was the juxtaposition under-pinning the war on terror.

A further significance of Mufti's life experience and pro-jihad is that he represents an important historical connection between the modern jihad and the Muslim anti-colonial experience of the Indian Sub-Continent. In a sense Mufti Abdul Rasheed illustrates a route to jihad which does not depend upon reading Syed Qutb and the Egyptian experience. As one of the intellectual influences on the Afghan Taliban Movement, Mufti Abdul Rasheed pulled them towards the cultural politics of Pakistan, India and the Dar ul Uloom Deoband. Such scholars and sponsors of the Taliban had learned a different history of struggles between Islam and its foes than that which was familiar to other admirers of the Taliban such as Osama bin Laden and Ayman al-Zawahiri. Mufti Rasheed was inspired by stories of Indian ulema who had fought and conspired against British colonial power. We can trace a direct connection between Mufti Rasheed and the most famous anti-British Indian Muslim endeavour, the Silk Letter Conspiracy. During the First World War a delegation of ulema travelled from Deoband to Kabul and proceeded to lobby the Afghan Amir Habibullah to allow Afghanistan to be used as a launching pad for a Turkish and German-backed revolt against British rule. The teacher who instructed Rasheed in the hadiths, whom Rasheed credits with inspiring his love of jihad, had in his youth voluntarily accompanied the convicted leaders of the Silk Letter Conspiracy to their three years of exile in Malta. Elements of the sub-continental route to jihad, intellectually pursued by Mufti Rasheed and his teachers, included identification of British power as a barrier to the supremacy of Islam, the need for alliances between Indian and Afghan Muslims to provide a base for jihad and the hope that they would find backing from the Istanbul-based Caliph. Mufti Rasheed, and those who followed the sub-continental route to jihad, dreamed of a global Islamic revival, with a role for the Caliph, but their main locus for action was in the Indian Sub-Continent and Afghanistan. Mufti Rasheed's engagement with the Afghan Taliban was in may ways a fulfilment of what his teacher and the Silk Letter conspirators had strived for.

2. SUMMARY OF HIS EDUCATION AND CAREER

Mufti Rasheed was born into a family with a strong tradition of Islamic scholarship, associated with the east Punjab town of Ludhiana. Ludhiana during the early nineteenth century served as a point of interface between India and Afghanistan because, after 1809, the British maintained a cantonment in the town. It was in Ludhiana that the deposed Afghan king Shah Shuja lived under British protection until the first Anglo-Afghan war 1838-1842. Mufti Rasheed's father however shifted to western Punjab, to Faisalabad and then Multan, districts which experienced rapid agricultural expansion in the first half of the twentieth century, as a result of the development of canal irrigation. Even after their migration and the subsequent partition of India, the family continued to celebrate their Ludhiana roots. In the case of Mufti Rasheed, this entailed adopting the epithet "Ludhianvi". The scholastic journey which commenced in Mian Channu, took Mufti Rasheed across Punjab and northern India. He followed the classic approach to acquisition of Muslim religious knowledge, migrating between madrassas, seeking out the teachers who would guide him through the books which encapsulated the Sunni tradition. Typically, Mufti Rasheed and students like him would spend one or two years in each place of study, usually taking a letter of recommendation to their next teacher and shifting in time to start classes in shawaal, the second month of the Islamic lunar calendar and the start of the madrassas' academic year.

Rasheed first studied in Gahuta Shareef, near Multan, where two of his brothers were already enrolled. There he commenced the *dars nizami*, the traditional Sunni madrassa curriculum, which was reformed and championed in India by the Dar ul Uloom Deoband. The curriculum provides for eight years of study, covering Arabic, theology, jurisprudence and history. In Gahuta he also started Persian, which had been the language of government of Muslim India, before it was displaced by English. He completed a year in Gahuta before shifting to Jehnagirabad to start studying Arabic and from there went to Darga Shareef and Gujrat to continue his *dars nizami*. Perhaps the most important stint of Rasheed's career as a student was the year 1941 to 1942, which he spent in the Dar ul Uloom, Deoband. The pinnacle of the *dars nizami* curriculum is normally the eighth year, devoted to comprehensive study of the hadiths. Rasheed was instructed by Syed Hussein Ahmad Madani, then Deoband's most distinguished Sheikh ul-Hadith. This course involved studying the main collections such as Bukhari, Muslim, Tirmizi and al-Nasai. Rasheed would draw on these extensively in his later writing.

Around the time of Rasheed's *daur e hadith*, his father shifted from Punjab to Sindh. Therefore, in 1943, after Deoband, Rasheed entered a madrassa in Hyderabad, Sindh, to commence his graduate studies. Alongside his studies, he started teaching hadiths from Sahih Bukari. He rapidly built a reputation for his command over the subject matter and was appointed director of the madrassa. This marked the start of his career as a recognised scholar. Now an accepted member of the ulema, Rasheed was talent-spotted and in 1957 he was invited to join the Dar ul Uloom Karachi as a Sheikh ul-Hadith. He served for a while as director of studies. But in an experience easily comprehensible to fellow academics, he found the administration too burdensome. He stepped down as director of studies so as to focus exclusively on his research and teaching. In his own continuing studies he qualified as a mufti, or one qualified to issue fatwas, statements of Islamic dogma applied to contemporary life. In 1962 Rasheed started to practice as a mufti, establishing a department (Dar ul-Ifta o Ershad) inside the Dar ul Uloom. But within a year he shifted out to establish his own institute, an independent madrassa built around a Dar ul-Ifta o Ershad. From 1963 until his death in 2002, Mufti Rasheed headed his own institutions, the madrassa and an Islamic welfare trust, which he built up around the Dar ul-Ifta o Ershad.

Rasheed's admirers are effusive in their praise of his personal qualities and his dogged pursuit of doctrinal traditionalism and social reform. They describe him as humble, pious, learned and yet passionate in his beliefs, persuasive as a teacher and forceful as an orator. He inspired tremendous loyalty among the followers he recruited through his preaching and they declared him one of the leading Islamic public intellectuals of his time. Mufti Rasheed took particular pride in the public lectures which he gave on Fridays and Sundays, during the 1970s. These, he asserted, had the power to transform lives once followers absorbed his vision of the role of the Muslim in modern society.

In his preaching, Mufti Rasheed was an ardent critic of modernity and of the impact of contact with the west on the lives of Muslims. After he had established himself as a senior member of the ulema, Rasheed harked back to the 1934 encounter and imagined his life as a riposte to the "gentleman" who had tried to "make me hate my religion". He said "if this gentleman were to see me today he would realise who is useless." Rasheed saw his success in his career as a triumph over the first westerner he encountered:

> "Thanks be to God, who has provided me everything in life and allowed me to live like a nawab. I am blessed with respect, and position. Above all, the riches which I was fated to enjoy include a calm in my heart, which no gentleman can ever dream of."

One of the traditions of the famous Islamic sages which Rasheed maintained was the interpretation of dreams. His ability to associate with prophets in his dreams enhanced Rasheed's image as a sage and spiritual figure. For example he relates a dream in which Mufti Rasheed undertook a pilgrimage and encountered a prophet with a stammer. He later determined that a stammer might be a sign of ability to access divine knowledge.

Rasheed's doctrinaire manner expressed itself in a rigid rejection of behaviours which he considered unIslamic. This gave rise to preoccupations which his admirers considered principled but his detractors considered dogmatic and rather eccentric. For example he steadfastly refused to let his picture taken, because of its association with polytheist worship of the graven image. The doctrinaire position pitted him against both westernised behaviour and un-Islamic traditions rooted in the social mores of the sub-continent (*urf*). For example, one of Mufti Rasheed's most famous fatwas addressed the issue of purdah within joint families. Rasheed decreed that a woman should maintain purdah from the brother of her husband. This contradicted the custom of north Indian Muslims. In communities where brothers and their wives lived together as joint families such an extension of purdah would be a major source of disruption in their lives.

Mufti Rasheed belonged to the generation who were already young adults at the time of partition of the sub-continent, so that they had both personal experience of the colonial encounter and spent most of their lives building the new countries. Rasheed's most immediate encounter with the political turmoil in the run up to independence came when his teacher of hadiths, Madani Sahib, was arrested by the British authorities and incarcerated in Muradabad jail. It was Madani who provided Rasheed his link to anti-colonial history. Madani Sahib's own teacher, Mehmud Hassan, erstwhile principal of Darul Uloom Deoband, had been one of the key figures who travelled to Kabul as part of the Silk Letter Conspiracy, before being arrested when the British authorities intercepted the conspirators' communications.

Although his own life was devoted to scholarship and teaching, Mufti Rasheed saw propagation of the idea of jihad as a central part of his persona. He writes of imbibing the spirit of jihad. He recalls that while studying hadiths in Deoband, he also received instruction in jihad. In part this involved the ideology of jihad and the history of the wars fought by the prophet and his companions. Madani Sahib and his books were Rasheed's main source of jihad-related inspiration. However Rasheed also describes how Deoband also provided more practical instruction in warfare from teachers such as Ustad Abdul Rahman and Ustad Abdul Rasheed. Mufti Rasheed also claimed a jihadi heritage in that he remembered his family as having supplied scholars to fight in successive rounds of jihad against the British. Muslim clerical-led or inspired resistance against British colonialism in India which Rasheed identified with included the campaign of Syed Ahmad Barelvi 1821-1831, the mujahideen movement in Malakand division after the death of Syed Ahmad, the "Indian mutiny" in 1857 and the Khilafat Movement in the 1920s. Rasheed was inspired by and linked to jihad as armed resistance to the British presence in India. He lectured on how the British sought to undermine Muslim civilization and political power through its colonial strategy, involving the spread of liberal education and western institutions. As a teacher propagating Islamic values and knowledge, Rasheed saw himself as participating in the resistance to this cultural imperialism. Propagation of violent jihad against the enemies of Islam simply represented an extension of that resistance. For Mufti Rasheed there was an essential unity between his lectures to families on how to live the Islamic good life and his work in propagating jihad from an Indian sub-continental perspective.

3. AL RASHEED TRUST AND THE AFGHAN TALIBAN

Rasheed's youth coincided with India's move to independence and a time when he and his peers could imagine a jihad against the British. However, by the time that Rasheed had become a senior cleric in Karachi, the modern jihad was being invented in Afghanistan. Rasheed was 56 by the time of the 1978 communist coup in Kabul which signalled the start of the violent conflict in that country and would have lasting global repercussions.

Karachi emerged as a significant hub for activities associated with the Afghan jihad, as ulema based in the city embraced the cause. The city's madrassas supplied fighters, Pakistani and international, to serve alongside Afghanistan's mujahideen parties. But a series of autonomous jihadi organisations were formed in Karachi, distinct from the Afghan jihadi parties, which were head-quartered in Peshawar. The Karachi parties went on to send groups to fight in the successive fronts of an emerging global jihad, which opened up beyond Afghanistan in the 1990s, including of course Kashmir, India and the Balkans. As Al-Qaeda emerged, some of its prominent figures spent part of their careers in Karachi, such as Khalid Sheikh Mohammad and Ilyas Kashmiri.

For most of his career, Mufti Rasheed extolled the idea of jihad and violent resistance to what he saw as a coordinated western effort to undermine Islamic civilisation without associating himself with any single jihadi party. However once the Taliban emerged in 1994, he proclaimed them to be the purest of jihadi groups yet to emerge and fully endorsed their struggle. One of the reasons for Rasheed's affinity for the Taliban may have been the movement's strong roots in the clergy. Those Afghan mujahideen parties with their roots in Ikhwan ul Musulmeen thought were largely run by men who had received a modern education rather than schooling in a madrassa. Furthermore, in terms of the austerity that they promoted in areas they captured, and the personal simplicity which their leader practised, the Taliban were much closer to the temperament of Rasheed himself than the ikhwani parties. Mufti Rasheed visited Afghanistan, met with Mullah Omar, travelled the country, and then tried to help the Taliban develop their dogma.

In the last decade of his life, Mufti Rasheed's practical engagement with the world of jihad expanded and acquired more a serious institutional foundation in a manner that should be regarded as a template for the role of Pakistan's senior jihadi clerics. In 1996, Rasheed founded Al Rasheed Trust.[3] Ostensibly this was an Islamic welfare organisation, collecting funds from zakaat and devoting them to worthy causes in Pakistan and the Muslim world. The Trust ran parallel to Rasheed's flagship organisation, the Dar ul-Ifta o Ershad and Rasheed headed both until his death. The Trust quickly established twenty-one branches across Pakistan and launched activities in conflict affected Muslim regions, including Afghanistan, Kosovo, Chechnya and Kashmir. It became one of the main conduits for Pakistani assistance to Taliban-ruled Afghanistan. Its declared humanitarian activities in Afghanistan included subsidised bakeries and mosque-building. By 2001 Mufti Rasheed and the leadership of the Trust considered the presence of the United Nations and humanitarian NGOs from western countries in Taliban-run Afghanistan to be an anomaly and a block to the progress of Islamisation. They manoeuvred to displace the World Food Programme as main provider of welfare assistance to vulnerable Afghans in Kabul and other cities. Tense negotiations between the UN and the Taliban, ensured that WFP supported bakeries stayed open, thus staving off the Rasheed Trust takeover attempt.[4] Conveying an idea of the order of magnitude of the Rasheed Trust operation, they claimed to supply materials amounting to the equivalent of one million dollars of humanitarian assistance to Afghanistan per week. However, Afghan Taliban veterans report that the Rasheed Trust's representatives developed a close relationship with the Taliban military. The Trust provided non-lethal materials and cash directly to the Taliban military, with the blessing of Mullah Omar. Testimony from Taliban veterans suggest that the assistance to the Taliban military was ultimately the most important aspect of its work in Afghanistan.

Rasheed and his associates also developed media organs to propagate their ideology of jihad. The most prominent of these has been Zarb-e-Momin, an Urdu language newspaper, which has provided a pro-Taliban and pro-jihad perspective on developments in Afghanistan and the world. Zarb-e-Momin is an example of the way in which pro-jihadi constituencies in Pakistan have sought to draw on the role models established by the Taliban and Al-Qaeda to inspire their own supporters in Pakistan. In this sense Rasheed and his outfits hoped to leverage the narrative of the Taliban's Islamic Emirate to help the cause of jihad in Pakistan. The publications also highlighted some of Rasheed's links within the broader Pakistani jihadi establishment. In particular, Zarb-e-Momin has periodically provided a platform to Masood Azhar, the founder of the Jaish Mohammad jihadi organisation, founded after he was freed through the hijacking of an Indian Airlines aircraft to Taliban-controlled Kandahar.

In October 1999, as part of the response to Al-Qaeda's international terror campaign, the United Nations Security Council adopted resolution 1267. This established a sanctions regime directed against Al-Qaeda and the Taliban Movement which was accused of hosting it. In 2001 the Al Rashid Trust was included in the list of entities which were subject to these sanctions. The formal listing accuses the trust of acting as a "financial facilitator" for Al-Qaeda and its related groups in Pakistan and Afghanistan, such as Jaish-i-Mohammad. The UN citation mentions that Al Rashid Trust operated in parallel to a similar Pakistan-based organisation, Al Akhtar Trust[5].

After Rasheed's death, he was succeeded by Mufti Abdul Raheem, a cleric brought up in Punjab who claims Afghan heritage. He operates from a well protected campus in Karachi, with madrassa and library and maintains links with key figures in the Taliban movement as part of the interface between Pakistan's jihadi establishment and the ongoing conflict in Afghanistan. Mufti Abdul Raheem has also been included on the UN sanctions list, accused of continuing the efforts to channel support to Al-Qaeda related groups.

II. Commentary on *Eta't Amir*

1. HOW THE TALIBAN USED MUFTI RASHEED'S *ETA'T AMIR* – OBEDIENCE TO THE LEADER

In the last year of the Taliban's government in Afghanistan, visitors to Mullah Omar's office in Kandahar received a parting gift. As they left, the movement's supreme leader asked them to take a slim volume from a pile beside the door. He told them that if they wanted to know how the Taliban were meant to behave, they should read the book. The books which Mullah Omar handed out were Pashto and Farsi translation of *Eta't Amir*, or obedience to the leader. Mufti Rasheed published the original in Urdu after having toured Taliban-run Afghanistan. Mullah Omar's endorsement indicates that he believed that Rasheed had captured the essence of the Taliban Movement.

Since the launch of the Movement there has been recurrent debate on the nature of Pakistani influence on the Taliban and the identity of the identity of Pakistani figures who have supported them. Afghans hostile to the Taliban have tended to focus on the role of prominent Pakistani religious party leaders Fazlur Rahman and Sami ul Haq and figures from the security establishment such as former Interior Minister Nasrullah Babar and retired intelligence operators Hameed Gul and Col. Imam. The way in which the Taliban embraced Mufti Rasheed's book, plus his direct dealings with the leadership and the material support he provided them through

Al Rasheed Trust, all suggest that Mufti Rasheed embodied the interaction between Pakistan and the Taliban.

The relationship between Mufti Rasheed was rather more subtle than the stories Taliban critics tend to tell about wicked spy-masters manipulating the movement. First of all, the relationship between the Taliban and Rasheed was founded on ideas, rather than merely transactions. Furthermore, keen as Rasheed was to instruct the Taliban on the correct Islamic way to run their movement, it is clear that ideas did not simply flow in one direction. Rasheed was inspired by what he saw of Taliban Afghanistan and then applied his reading of the Deobandi religio-political tradition to offer them detailed guidance. As many members of the movement had themselves studied in Deobandi madrassas, they were already familiar with the sources Rasheed drew on. The Taliban's own later efforts to codify acceptable behaviour for their fighters and officials, particularly their lahya reproduce some of Rasheed's guidelines, but without acknowledging him as a source.

2. *ETA'T AMIR* AS A GUIDE TO TALIBAN INTERNAL DOCTRINE

The main reason that Eta't Amir deserves to be read is that it provides insights into the rationale for some of the characteristic aspects of the Taliban organisational culture.[6] The Taliban rapidly adopted a distinctive approach to internal organisation, which set the movement apart from the multiple other political and military organisations which have emerged during the Afghan conflict. In many ways the Taliban have behaved as advocated by Rasheed, even if he was not the only teacher who could claim credit for their organisational effectiveness.

The Afghan Taliban Movement has maintained an organisational culture, during the different phases of its development which sets it apart from other political and military organisations in the country. Indeed, it is this organisational approach which is distinctive rather than the objectives which the movement has articulated. Neither is opposition to the presence of foreign military forces exceptional within Afghan politics, nor is the demand for application of Islamic shariat law. The jihadi parties which now form part of the political establishment in Kabul have all articulated these demands in one form or another. The Taliban's contribution to the conflict in Afghanistan has been the demonstration of a robust organisational model apparently resistant to the hazards or splits and patronage politics, which have weakened other Islamist organisations' pursuit of their goals.

The central element of the Taliban organisational culture is their leadership cult, centred around the idea of Mullah Omar as Amir ul-Mu'mineen, leader of the faithful. The main focus of Rasheed's book is the role of the leader and his subordinate amirs. Rasheed uses multiple hadith to establish obedience to their amir as a religious duty for the Taliban. He tells the Taliban that submission to the authority of their amir is essential to comply with the prophet's instructions for leading the Muslim community after his death.

As well as the enduring high status of the Taliban's leader, the movement has operated in a remarkably centralised manner. Most accessible officials profess that they have no authority as decisions are made at a higher level, there is a profound lack of transparency and even the much discussed leadership shura has rarely seemed able to make decisions. Most recently, in early 2015, analysts of the Taliban tried to make sense of a seemingly vital shura meeting in Karachi. This supposedly addressed the existential issue of talk or fight but ended with an agreement to refer the matter to the leader. Rasheed's doctrine provides a rationale both for acceptance of leadership decisions handed down to the base and for the marginal consultative role of a shura. He also provides arguments to deter dissent and splits, which have both been rare, during the Taliban's twenty year record of cohesiveness.

Several more specific aspects of organisational practice, which have long been noticed by Taliban watchers, receive a treatment. Both in their period running a government and during the insurgency, the Taliban have blurred the distinction between civilian and military appointments. While they were in power, even senior figures whose primary appointments were in civilian roles in the ministries, would periodically absent themselves, to spend time on the battle-front. Rasheed rationalises this by referring to the need to reacquaint office-bound personnel with the glories of jihad and sacrifice, to ensure that they not stray from the original spirit of the movement. The movement has also practised frequent rotations in its appointments, especially at the mid level, with provincial governors and officials in ministries or commissions typically replaced after a year. These appointments are made without observance of hierarchical progression and with little sign of the kind of entrenched local interest that the Kabul government has grappled with in appointments. Even senior figures have accepted periods without an appointment or have returned to office at a lower level than that at which they previously served. All of this is in keeping with Rasheed's guidelines for running the Islamic movement.

The movement has also, throughout its existence, sustained a culture which is simultaneously cliquish, overtly pious and Spartan. There has been no move towards diversity as the Taliban has sustained its identity as a movement of religious students and clerics. All communications of the movement are replete with religious references and in their personal dealings, Taliban commanders and officials typically present themselves as pious individuals. Rasheed stresses the importance of reinforcing piety within the movement as one of the ways that the Islamic movement can avoid the failures which have beset its predecessors. He also specifically addresses the perils of trappings of office and wealth, arguing that allowing officials to enjoy wealth and luxury would subvert the movement's central authority and weaken the commitment to jihad. The movement has also consistently proclaimed itself to be above tribal and clan identity, stressing only its Islamic identity. Internal critics of the Taliban have complained of creeping clannishness, especially the concentration of power in the hands of a faction in the Ishaqzai. However Taliban rhetoric has always condemned ethnic division and Rasheed provides arguments relating this to the central purpose of maintaining cohesiveness of the Islamic movement.

Finally, another enduring aspect of the Taliban organisational culture is that the movement is tangibly Afghan. Critics of the movement have periodically tried to establish that its primary cultural influences are located in Pakistan and have theorised that boys brought up in madrassas in that country are insulated from the socialisation which occurs in the Afghan village. But, on the contrary, in its political stance the Taliban movement has always articulated an agenda for Afghanistan and leadership figures have remained preoccupied with the many unsettled issues of the Afghan civil war. And despite the official rhetoric abjuring tribalism and clannishness, Taliban have long drawn upon Afghan cultural resources such as using tribal networks to mobilise support for their fighters. Although Rasheed does not explicitly address the issue of Afghaniat, or the Afghan identity of the Taliban, Rasheed can be thought of as belonging to a long cultural-historical tradition of sub-continental Islamists looking to Afghanistan as a source of an unadulterated Islam backed by military force.

3. HOW THE TALIBAN INSPIRED MUFTI RASHEED

A reading of *Eta't Amir* immediately reveals that Rasheed was not so much impressed by the Taliban as inspired by them. Perhaps the most telling phrase is where he proclaims that countless sages have gone to their graves dreaming of that which he has had the privilege to witness – the rise of the Taliban Movement.

Rasheed emphasises the humble origins of the men who make up the movement. In this there is little doubt that he felt a particular affinity as he too had served as a poor student, moving from madrassa to madrassa in search of respected teachers. In this sense there was a continuity between Rasheed's first train journey and the mission of Mullah Omar and his companions.

Rasheed explicitly praises the Taliban for the long list of supposedly corrupt social practices which they banned, from alcohol to television or usury as well as rejoicing that they have had the courage to implement hudood punishments, by executing adulterers. In latter years, some Taliban spokesmen have referred to their early excesses and implied that a future Taliban dispensation might moderate its social policy. But Rasheed, who had a personal reputation for leading an austere life, celebrated the Taliban's clamp down as part of the return to true Islam, which he and his peers had never achieved in Pakistan.

Another striking feature of Rasheed's rhetoric is his references to archaic enemies. For example, the forces aligning in the global conspiracy against the Taliban and Islam include polytheists and Manichaeans. Invoking resistance to Manichaeanism seems somewhat esoteric, given that this middle eastern religion has been essentially extinct for nearly a millennium. However the Taliban inspire in Rasheed a vision of the early expansion of Islam. He therefore invokes some of those forces which the first generations of Muslims confronted. Taliban actions soon after Rasheed published invoked similar symbols in a most practical way, when Mullah Omar decreed that they must destroy idols. Although it is hard to find manifestations of Manichaeanism in the modern world, Bamyan is one of the site which was associated by the founder of the religion, Mano. In Rasheed's imagination, while destroying the Buddhas of Bamyan, the Taliban were not just destroying idols but erasing the influence of Manichaeanism.

Observers struggled to explain why a movement in the twenty first century should prioritise actions against religious artefacts which had not been worshipped for centuries. However Rasheed's writing may suggest a logic. The organisational guidance which Rasheed offers to the Taliban and which fairly well describes their actual political practice, is firmly based on his reading of the conduct of the earliest Muslim leaders and their armies. The main body of examples which he draws on to instruct the Taliban is a set of forty hadith, all of which refer to the conduct of the prophet of Islam and his companions. He constructs from these practical advice on how to run a movement, drawing no doubt on the instruction which he received from the anti-British revolutionaries in the Deoband seminary. The references to polytheists and Manichaeans help to invoke the struggles of those early Muslims, reinforcing the message that the Taliban are their heirs and should heed their lessons on how to run a movement.

4. *ETA'T AMIR* AND THE IDEA OF RESISTANCE TO THE WEST

Rasheed's commentary on and advice to the Taliban provides insights into how a prominent Pakistani Islamist relates the politico-religious struggle in Afghanistan to his world-view. In his foreword he roundly condemns the erstwhile leaders of the Afghan anti-Soviet jihad as having betrayed the Islamic movement, naming both Hekmatyar and Rabbani. This much is unremarkable, given that from the outset the Taliban based their claim to legitimacy on the notion that the older jihadi parties had plunged the country into anarchy. However Rasheed introduces a rather different criticism. He considers Hekmatyar and Rabbani traitors to the Islamic movement because they strayed from the true path of Islamisation by adopting western political nomenclature and institutions in their attempt to re-establish government in Afghanistan after capturing Kabul in 1992. He looks to the Taliban to implement their system of Emirate, with all authority resting in the rightly-guided ruler, as a counter-point both to the errant mujahideen leaders and to what he considered as the corrosive influence of western-style political institutions. This visceral hostility to a democratic political order indicates the ambiguous position figures such as Rasheed have found themselves in while operating in Pakistan. They have somehow managed to position themselves as simultaneously a part of the establishment, aligned with its security institutions, while rejecting the very basis of the political order.

Rasheed's commentary also provides a classic and rather colourful example of denunciation of the western conspiracy against Islam in general and the Taliban in particular. The context in which Rasheed wrote was the pre-9/11 world, with the Taliban in power in Kabul, but under United Nations and United States sanctions. Al-Qaeda had launched its initial attacks, in particular the East Africa embassy bombings. Pakistan's religious right had mobilised a "Defence of Afghanistan Committee", which vowed to save the Taliban and thwart UN personnel implementing their arms embargo. (There were of course no such personnel as it is member states, such as Pakistan, which implement UN sanctions resolutions). Rasheed warned the Taliban that the West and the global anti-Islam forces could not tolerate their implementation of the Shariat and were therefore bound to try to thwart the process. He thus argued that the process of trying to implement Shariat within Afghanistan inevitably drew the Taliban into a global confrontation. This position deliberately avoids engaging with the rationale that the US and the UN Security Council eventually offered for the international intervention in Afghanistan – the Taliban hosting of international terrorists, which constituted a threat to international security under chapter seven of the UN Charter. Rasheed's formula has endured. Pakistani Islamists have consistently characterised the 2001 intervention in Afghanistan as having been motivated by a desire to reverse the Taliban's implementation of the Shariat. The Taliban Movement in its official publications has also preferred this explanation of why international forces came to Afghanistan, thus declining to acknowledge that it could have been a response to terrorist attacks.

Rasheed's rhetoric about the convergence of anti-Shariat forces deliberately links the Taliban's local action within Afghanistan with Rasheed's idea of global Islamic resistance. Although the Taliban themselves have consistently denied any ambitions beyond Afghanistan, Rasheed and his heirs tried to build up a support infrastructure which would allow them to engage with other mujahideen whom they saw as participating in that global resistance.

5. A NOTE ON MUFTI RASHEED'S SOURCES

Mufti Rasheed mainly draws on the classic hadith collections which he would have become familiar with during his madrassa training, in which he followed the sub-continental *dars nizami* course. The majority of the references which he gives are to books which he would have become familiar with during his study of the hadith in Deoband. However Mufti Rasheed demonstrates that he is widely read in the hadith by citing multiple additional collections, beyond those included in the core *dars nizami* curriculum. Mufti

Rasheed liberally cites the "six books" (kutub al-sitta), which constitute the core of Sunni hadith scholarship – the *sahih bukhari* of Mohammad al-Bukhari, the *sahih muslim* of Muslim ibn al-Hajjaj, the *sunan al-sughra* of Al-Nasai, the *sunan abu daoud* of Abu Daoud, the *sunan al-tirmizi* of Al-Tirmizi and the *sunan ibn majah* of Ibn Majah. From the Six Books he relies mainly on Bukhari and Muslim. Alongside these core texts, the collection which he refers to most frequently is the musnad of Ahmad Ibn Hanbal. Other texts from which he draws hadith include the sunan al-kubra of al-Bayhaqi, the collections of Abu al-Qasim Sulaiman Ibn Ahmad Ibn al-Tabarani and the al-mowatta of Imam Malik and Abu Malik al-Harith bin Asim al-Ashari. Rasheed deliberately bases his study on what he considers to be authentic descriptions of the life and times of the Prophet Mohammad by restricting himself to the accepted primary sources. The only citations which he gives are for his eleven quotes from the Koran and for his extensive use of the hadith. Rasheed prefers not to rely on scholars from the past millennium as the scholars he draws on date from the early Muslim era – Ibn Hanbal A.D. 780-855, Imam Bukhari A.D. 810 – 870 and Muslim AD 817 to 874.

III. English translation of *Eta't Amir*

ETA'T AMIR – OBEDIENCE TO THE LEADER

Important instructions and sayings of the Prophet for the Prophet's army, the Taliban mujahideen.

Foreword

We cannot praise god enough for the fact that after so long he has blessed the oppressed Muslim nation by granting a new Emirate and Islamic government in the pattern of the rightly guided caliphs. Thousands of Islamic scholars have left this world still cherishing the wish that they should see such a phenomenon.

Oh how many desires have been buried in the grave

It is god's great blessing that the Amir ul-Mu'mineen and the madrassa students, after great sacrifice and expending their pure, precious blood, have brought peace to our hearts. Our proud and spiritual sons have implemented Islamic laws the law of God and thrown dust on the propaganda of the atheists, Manicheans, Jews and Christians that the system based on the Koran and hadith is outdated and cannot actually be put into practice. The system based on the Koran and the Hadith has become reality. It was impossible to hide this from society. It is a shame that this shameless futile propaganda had caused the weaker sort of Muslims to lose their way. The implementation of Islam had become an ancient tale. Some of those who were taking the name of Islam were using it for their own vested and political interests, while in Kabul even those veteran leaders of the fourteen year struggle had achieved power and all pomp and glory. But, instead of applying the true Islam they were busy with a fake Islam. They had adopted the unIslamic terms of democracy, president and prime minister and interim president and minister and elections and so were following the way of America and Europe in the guise of Islam. They had become like the meaning of this verse

He did the Haj at the Kaaba and bathed in the Ganges
Keeping God happy and the devil satisfied as well

Hekmatyar, Ahmad Shah Masood, Rabbani and Sayyaf's disloyalty to Islam, and their treachery to the sacred blood of sixteen hundred thousand martyrs did so much damage to Islam and Muslims. They defamed jihad throughout the world. They damaged the whole jihadi movement. What they did to upset peace and security, defy the divine orders and trample on all that is sacred cannot be expressed. But eventually, God in his mercy and pride was fired up to implement his system through the hands of weak, powerless, inexperienced and humble madrassa students.

And so because today Islam is fully implemented throughout an area amounting to four hundred and fifty thousand square kilometres, the hudood, qisas and other shariat punishments are in force. In Kandahar city an adulterer and adulteress and fornicators have been stoned to death. That system which for ages had been confined to books and merely decorated the cupboards and libraries has now, thank God, been implemented. If in today' world Judaism and Christianity are applied in a corrupt and altered shape, at least we Muslims can hold our heads high and proclaim that today Islam is applied in its true and original form.

Through the blessings of the Taliban's Islamic system and shariat based emirate, the land of the martyrs has been cleansed of all wrong doings and crimes. Shamelessness, obscenity and immodesty have been ended. Singing, music, dance and beard trimming and cutting have been banned.

Possessing and watching TV, VCRs and dish antennas have been made into an unpardonable crimes. Alcohol and kebabs, pictures, insurance, interest and gambling have all been made illegal. Peace and justices have been achieved by ending theft, armed robbery and oppression. Shariat courts have been established with provide the people with instant justice. All oppressive taxes have been banned and instead the system of ushr and zakat has been introduced.

The name of God and the divine system have been proclaimed and all of Satan's ways and system have been brought low and buried. The sympathy and prayers of every Muslim are now with these daring pioneers of Islam, the Taliban.

When I travelled to Kandahar and Herat and witnessed the sheer joy of faith and Islam, I recalled the famous verse:

For they are my sons, bring back those in the likeness of my sons

Spontaneously I found on my lips the words:

For they are my fathers, bring back those in the likeness of my fathers

What is obvious is that as long as the Taliban maintain their self-sacrificial spirit, matchless fervour and sincerity of purpose and their internal consensus and unity, then the largest or strongest enemy can do nothing to destroy the Islamic government. But if God forbid, disagreements and splits were to develop then, even without a confrontation, this great blessing can be destroyed.

You will move the heavens, turn the earth upside down
You are the powerless, were you to all make your voices into one voice

COMING TO THE POINT

It is well known to all organs of the Islamic movement of the Taliban – its shura, provincial governors, district administrators, judges and commanders, that, faced with the martyrdom, selflessness, spirit, sincerity, unity and love of the Taliban, the whole infidel world has been rendered powerless and humbled and has taken up arms. As long as there is love and sincerity, the army of the prophet has will be victorious. But this has forced the enemy to scheme and think of such plots. If we do not find a direct and appropriate defence against this plot, then once more Islam will be targeted by the enemy's destructive force.

The plot is an attempt one way or another to create differences and splits within the ranks of the army of the prophet, the Taliban. The enemy will infiltrate its agents into this sacred movement. It will create misunderstanding and suspicion. The enemy will try to take advantage of some people's weakness, their lack of tolerance, their prejudice. Using those who do not even have a moderate level of honesty or religious understanding they will try to exploit their cowardice and spread difference. In such a situation I have found it necessary to share with every worker, large or small, engaged in this great jihad, the orders of god, the blessed teaching of his prophet and the texts of our Muslim community, so that they may stay safe from from the scheming of the enemy, especially the hidden enemy, and defy the intentions of Satan.

I hope that the Taliban, who, after ages, have achieved this great feat of establishing the Islamic caliphate and confining the plans of the infidels to the dust, will now listen carefully to this advice, or rather to this testament. They should all put it into practice so that even the most junior person in the Taliban will not allow himself to become the first brick of a conspiracy against Islam.

Section One

MAINTAINING INTERNAL CONSENSUS AND UNITY AND AVOIDING DIFFERENCES AND SPLITS

The Taliban have implemented a supreme and sacred system in the land of the martyrs, the ultimate authority of which is the god of the martyrs and mujahideen. This same authority has given so much attention to establishing the maintenance of consensus and unity as a duty and has rendered the propagation of difference as reprehensible and most unfortunate. The relevant instructions are:

THE FOUNDATIONS OF RELIGION ARE INCOMPATIBLE WITH DIFFERENCES

“Allah set that religion for you which was brought to you by the prophet Noah, the same which was sent to you through the prophets Abraham, Moses and Jesus. They carried the instruction to you that you must hold fast to this religion and never oppose it.” (Qur’an 42:13).[7,8]

Two important issues have been shown in this Ayat

1. The instruction to maintain consensus and unity is so important and great that it has been delivered to the most honourable prophets and their peoples. The whole value of the shariat is linked to this instruction.

2. The foundations of religion are impossible without consensus and unity.

This shows that if someone through his deeds or words gives rise to dissent, then in reality he is acting against Islam and is showing defiance to Islam.

POWER AND GRANDEUR ARE LOST THROUGH DIFFERENCE

"And obey Allah and His Apostle and do not quarrel for then you will be weak in hearts and your power will depart, and be patient; surely Allah is with the patient". (Qur'an 8:46).[9]

Several issues are shown by this:

Benefits

1. Your power will dissipate from internal difference, through which the enemy will unexpectedly lose his fear. As an ultimate consequence of this Islam will be destroyed.

2. The secret formula for maintaining internal consensus and unity in any social endeavour is that if you face something which is counter to your opinion, nature or advice, then you should put on a show of patience.

3. If this patience seems to you like an effort and a burden then trust in God's company, the god of the patient. Tell yourself that this divine company is no ordinary treasure.

The instruction of God's messenger:

From Bokari, Muslim and Ahmad[10]

"If a decision of your amir seems unpleasant then show patience"

AVOIDING THE STINKING THOUGHTS OF PARTY MANOEUVRING, TRIBALISM AND BIGOTRY

"And hold fast by the covenant of Allah all together and be not disunited, and remember the favour of Allah on you when you were enemies, then He united your hearts so by His favor you became brethren; and you were on the brink of a pit of fire, then He saved you from it, thus does Allah make clear to you His communications that you may follow the right way." (Qur'an 3:103).[11]

Benefit: in this too some aspects are worth noting.

1. This ayat is fully applicable to the Taliban and therefore the Taliban should read the text of this ayat again and again. There was a time when the Taliban were divided into various groups and there was no possibility of them working together. But God was kind and under his name and his plan all the groups united under the amir and became as one and indistinguishable from each other and freed from the dirt of organisational difference and were cleansed of group prejudice and hatred and were bathed in sweetness and love. In this way the idols of party manoeuvring, ethnicity and bigotry were broken and all memory of barbarism were erased.

2. If at any time the devil tempts you, dwell on the words "jal-allah" and think how can I do the bidding of the wretched satan rather than the bidding of God?

3. To maintain sweetness and love it has been commanded that the great blessing of unity be discussed and God be thanked for this for from one blessing one progresses to another blessing.

If you are thankful then more blessings will be showered upon you.

And discuss this and debate upon issues that unite you and avoid bringing divisive issues into discussion.

The demon of tribalism, clannishness, regionalism and factionalism is injurious to both this world and religion. In this regard certain actions are obligatory.

1. Every member of the movement should pay particular attention to the fact that the heart and mind should be kept free of any form of prejudice. In involuntarily such a thought comes to mind, it should never be translated into words.

2. If some action provokes such suspicion, then recite three times "God protect me from satan", turn to your left and say "thoo, thoo" and believe that this action has been undertaken in good faith based upon authority. Tell yourself that at the most this is an error of the amir in his striving, which will not be considered a sin for him, rather he will be rewarded.

3. Remember that harbouring suspicion is a major sin and a precursor to other major sins. Harbouring suspicion can destroy any social endeavour. It is a grave misdemeanour to harbour suspicions about your amir, based upon rumours or scruples and without shariat based reason.

THE SECRET FORMULA FOR AVOIDING EVERY ERROR

"Do not become like those people who after the arrival of the clear instructions divided themselves with differences, as for those people the day will be a great torment when some faces are made white and some faces are made black." (Qur'an 3:105, 106).[12]

Benefit

1. This ayat, just like the first ayat one hundred percent applies to the condition of the Taliban. Taking into account the place and situation this ayat is so important for the Taliban that it has the potential to protect them from every mistake and to warn them of any danger. Likewise if the Taliban fail to pay attention to the lesson of this ayat then they will be vulnerable to every danger.

Every office member of the Taliban movement should fix this in his mind that there were other mujahideen before them upon whom God bestowed the treasure of jihad in the way of God. As a result of this the Soviet Union was destroyed. Allah granted them force, suzerainty and power. But they did not value this and instead of implementing Islam they succumbed to internal differences. Not only did the wretched results render them infamous throughout the world, jihad, which is a sacred duty in Islam, also got a bad name.

If those to whom the Taliban's sacred movement is entrusted do not learn a lesson from the fate of the previous people, then listen, their fate will be no different from the fate of the previous people, rather it will be worse than their fate. From those people's differences only the section of jihad was affected. But if the Taliban fall prey to differences it will bring a bad name to the whole of Islam. Islamic affairs and the sacredness of God's name and his system will be trodden underfoot.

DISSENT IS THE WORK OF POLYTHEISTS

"Do not become polytheists – those people who have brought splits in their religion" (Qur'an 30:31, 32).[13]

Benefit

1. This shows that in the Koran indulging in difference and divergence is the work of the polytheists.

It is a shame that the matter has been turned upside down. Now the infidels and polytheists observe the instruction of the Koran to maintain strict unity and consensus. Despite the differences arising from their varying colours, races, languages, temperaments, interests, concerns, in their confrontation with the Muslims they are united and of one mind on every front. Meanwhile the Muslims have neglected this instruction and have descended to tearing each other apart and destroying Islam.

MAINTAINING CONSENSUS AND UNITY IS VERY DEAR TO GOD

"Allah holds dear to him those people who follow his path and maintain unity while they fight, as if they were a single edifice." (Qur'an 61:4).[14]

Benefit

1. Who can deny the importance of that action which renders someone dear to Allah?

Section Two

OBEDIENCE TO THE AMIR

This testament is so important and great that it is appropriate, even important, to describe it as the summary or essence of this guidance.

Acting upon this testament will be the guarantee of the welfare of the Taliban Islamic Movement, in this world and the next. Closing every door to difference will keep flowing the spring of familiarity and love between the leadership and the junior-most member of the Taliban.

Oh God's brave mujahideen, selfless Taliban, the Koran, hadith and common sense show that in organisational matters, in anything which involves a collective task, obedience to the amir is as important as air and breathing are to staying alive.

Come self-sacrificing army of Mohammad!

Obedience to the Amir is the order obedience to which distinguishes either the highest office holder or the junior most member as sincere and faithful.

This is the criterion which distinguishes jihad, the supreme act of worship, from discordant politics. It was on this scale that the sincerity of the rightly guided caliphs' governors, ministers and commanders was weighed. It is through this pulse that the doctor diagnoses a disease.

This is that same secret which in the first century made Islam honoured in four sixths of the world and won for it power, majesty and reverence. It is that true brightness which made Rome and Persia and their great powers scatter before a few humble hut dwellers. It was this which made the tallest, most robust and strongest abodes of the infidels and polytheism come tumbling onto the ground with a crash. Every member of the Taliban movement, whether he be a member of the shura, or a provincial governor, or a soldier on the battlefield, or someone following orders in an office, must act with this in mind, that any deficiency occurring in the Obedience to the Amir is tantamount to a deficiency in Islam.

Any weakening of the spirit of observance of Obedience to the Amir weakens the implementation of God's system. Therefore God has linked Obedience to the Amir to obedience to God and his prophet.

GOD'S TEACHING:

["O you who believe! obey Allah and obey the Apostle and those in authority from among you"; (Qur'an 4:59).][15]

The prophet also has left us numerous hadith in which he defined obedience to the amir as a duty and in different ways showed its importance.

FORTY HADITH

First Hadith

The Prophet (PBUH) spake thus:

Whoever has obeyed me he has certainly obeyed God.
Whoever has disobeyed me he has certainly disobeyed God.
Whoever has obeyed his Amir, he has certainly obeyed me.
Whoever has disobeyed his Amir, he has definitely disobeyed me.
(From Bukhari, Muslim and Ahmad)

Benefit

Those who oppose the Amir, should fear the wrath of Allah, because this is tantamount to opposing the prophet, which is such a very dangerous and fearsome act.

And to those fortunates who obey the Amir, countless felicitations, because they are, in fact, obeying the Prophet.

Second Hadith

The Prophet (PBUH) spake thus:

"Listen to the Amir's orders and obey the Amir even if an Abyssinian slave whose head is scrunched up like a raisin has been appointed as Amir over you."
(From Bukhari)

Third Hadith

The Prophet (PBUH) spake thus:

"Listen to the orders of the Amir and obey him, in easy times and in difficulty, in happiness and in hardship and even when someone else is given preference over you."

(From Muslim, Al-Nisai, Ahmad, Al-Majah)

In other words obedience to the amir is necessary under all circumstances, whether it seems easy or hard and pleasant or unpleasant, even if despite you being deserving, someone else gets preference.

Fourth Hadith

The Prophet (PBUH) spake thus:

"It is the duty of a Muslim to listen carefully to the orders of the Amir and to obey them whether it agrees with his temperaments or not. Excepting only if the order is a sin then he may they not listen to it for in this case it justifiable to disobey."

(From Bukhari, Muslim, Ibn Daud)

It is established in the Koran and the hadith and religious consensus that obedience to the order of the Amir is obligatory as long as he does not give an order counter to shariat, otherwise.

Obedience to none of God's creatures justifies disobedience to the Creator.

Fifth Hadith

The Prophet (PBUH) spake thus:

"Whoever has given allegiance to the Amir and given his hand in the hand of the Amir, and who has presented his heartfelt love in the Amir's service, he should show absolute obedience to the Amir, unless the Amir starts to fight some other Amir over the Emirate. In that case, behead him."

(From Muslim)

You can gauge the emphasis on obedience to the Amir ul-Mu'mineen is such that it extends to an order to kill anyone who seeks to usurp him.

Sixth Hadith

Hazrat Salma (RATA) said to the Holy Prophet (PBUH)

"O prophet of god! If our Ameers demand from us that which is due to them but do not give to us that which is due to us, then what the orders for us? The prophet evaded them in such a way that only after asking again and yet again, would they understand the importance of the reply. They asked a second time and according to some traditions a third time. Then You (The Holy Prophet PBUH) told them listen to the order of the Amir and obey it, for the Amir will answer for his actions and you will answer for yours."

(From Muslim)

Seventh Hadith

"Hazrat Arbaz bin Saria (RATA) says that one day after the Fajr (dawn) prayer, the prophet started to preach in such a way that eyes filled with tears and hearts throbbed. One man said to him, oh prophet, this seems like a farewell sermon. So what special command would you have for us when you depart this world?

The Prophet said : I bequeath to you that you should avoid disobeying God and should listen to and obey (the orders of the Amir)".

(From Al-Ajari)

Some traditions also say:

"In religious matters follow what I and the rightly guided caliphs did. In administrative matters obey the orders of the Amir, even if he is an Abyssinian slave. Hold onto this testament tightly".

Eighth Hadith

The Prophet (PBUH) spake thus:

"I give you orders for five things. Listen to the orders of the Amir and obey him, remain a member of the community. Do hijrat and jihad."

(From Bukhari, Bin Asim)

Ninth Hadith

The Prophet (PBUH) spake thus:

"After me, decisions will have to be made on behalf of the community. And these tasks also which you may consider superficial. The Sahaba (Companions of the Prophet, RATA) asked Oh prophet, if any of us should experience such a period, what command do you have for us?

You must fulfil the responsibility that is their due to them as their right, that is their orders. And you seek what is due to you as your right, from God."

(From Bukhari, Muslim)

This shows that if in someone's opinion someone else has been given preferential treatment, rather than making a noise about it, he should turn his attention to god, and pray. The hearts of the authorities and the Ameers and all treasures are fully in the control of God's powers.

Tenth Hadith

The Prophet (PBUH) spake thus:

"Undoubtedly there will be no prophet after me nor will there be any community of believers after you. Beware! Worship your god and say your five daily prayers. Keep your Ramadan fasts and wholeheartedly give zakaat on your wealth. Obey your Ameers. Through this you will gain admission to your god's paradise."

(From Tirmizi, Bin Asim)

Eleventh Hadith

The Prophet (PBUH) spake thus:

"A congregation is a blessing and solitude is a curse."
(From Bin Asim, Ibn Hanbal)

Twelfth Hadith

Hazrat Omar relates that the Holy Prophet stood amidst us and said:

"Whoever wishes to enter within Paradise must stay with the community."
(From Bin Asim, Ibn Askari, Tareekh Damishq, Tareekh Baghdad)

Thirteenth Hadith

The Prophet (PBUH) spake thus:

"You must consider it essential to hold fast to your community and avoid separation. Those of you who want to go to heaven should hold tight to your community."
(Ibn Hanbal, Tirmizi, Bukhari)

Fourteenth Hadith

The Prophet (PBUH) spake thus:

"God looked after the children of Israel. When one prophet died another would take his place. But after me there will be no more prophets."
Then a man asked, what will happen after you?
The instruction says:
"There will be caliphs and many of them"
He said "Oh prophet, what will be your command for that time?"
"give the allegiance that you gave before, and after that, as before, give them their due (that is obey them) And if he does not give you your due, do not make a fuss about it because God will question him (them) about your rights."
(From Bukhari, Muslim, Ahmad)

This hadith proves that the Islamic Shara'i Amir is a the vice-regent of the Prophet.

Fifteenth Hadith

"Whichever Amir is appointed over you, listen to what he says and obey him."
(From Ibn Asim)

Sixteenth Hadith

The Prophet (PBUH) spake thus:

“I am giving you commands regarding five matters, which commands God himself gave me. passed onto me as an order. Stay with the congregation. Listen to what the amir says. Obey the amir. Do hijrat and do jihad in the path of god. He who strays from the congregation/community even the distance of a hand-span, he has cast off the yoke of Islam from his neck until such time as he having repented returns.

And he who has raised the slogans of barbarism, for example tribalism or factionalism, then he is from the groups going to hell.

Someone asked, “Even if he is attentive to his prayers and fasting?”

Reply: “Even so he will be from the groups going to hell”

Oh god’s people! Take the names that god has given you. He has named you Muslims and believers.”

Another tradition says:

“Whoever strays even one bow’s length from the congregation, neither his prayers nor his fasts will be accepted. Such people will be the fuel of Hell’s eternal fire”.
(From Ahmad, Ashari)

Seventeenth Hadith

The Prophet (PBUH) spake thus:

"There are three people whom god will not ask about, (i.e. not show them the slightest compassion or love.) The first of these is the person who chooses to separate from the congregation and in so doing disobeys the prayer leader and then dies in this state of disobedience."

(From Ahmad)

Eighteenth Hadith

The Prophet (PBUH) spake thus:

"I command you three things.

1. Worship God and do not involve anyone else with him
2. Hold tightly to the rope of God and do not oppose
3. Obey the Amir whom god has appointed over you."

(From Malik, Ahmad, Bukhari)

Nineteenth Hadith

The Prophet (PBUH) spake thus:

"Listen with attention to what the amir says and obey him in all circumstances. Whether you are in easy circumstances or difficulty, whether happy or sad, even if someone has been preferred over you, do not hesitate from obeying the amir. Even if the Ameers grab your wealth, or flog your back relentlessly, then still obey them until it is a rebellion, because obedience in a rebellion it is not right."

(From Al-Bayhaqi, Bukhari)

Twentieth Hadith

Hazrat Umm-i- Hussain (RATA) said:

"On the Last Haj, I was with the prophet, of the many commands You (the Prophet PBUH) told me, one special command was that
Even if an ugly black slave is appointed over you as amir, who guides you by the book of god, you should listen to what he says and obey him."
(From Muslim, Ahmad)

Twenty-First Hadith

The Prophet (PBUH) spake thus:

"On the day of judgement those people who have obeyed their amir will face no charges, while those who have heard their amir and disobeyed him will find no support from anyone."
(From Ibn Asim, Behaqi, Tirmizi)

Twenty-Second Hadith

The Prophet (PBUH) spake thus:

"God's help is with the congregation while Satan is with them who oppose the congregation, and obstruct it."
(From Al-Tibrani)

Twenty-Third Hadith

"Whoever leaves the congregation and shows contempt for the authority of the emirate, God will meet with him in such a situation that he will have no standing."
(From Ahmad)

Twenty-Fourth Hadith

The Prophet (PBUH) spake thus:

“Whoever find the amir’s instructions unacceptable, he should be patient because whoever strays even on hand span from the Imam, he will die the barbaric death of an infidel.”

(From Bukhari, Muslim, Ahmad)

Twenty-Fifth Hadith

The Prophet (PBUH) spake thus:

“Whoever strays from obedience to the amir and separates from the congregation, he will die the barbaric death of an infidel.”

(From Ibn Asim)

Twenty-Sixth Hadith

The Prophet (PBUH) spake thus:

“He who strays even one hand span from the congregation, he has removed the yoke of Islam from around his neck.”

(From Abu Daoud, Ahmad, Ibn Asim)

Twenty-Seventh Hadith

The Prophet (PBUH) spake thus:

“Who ever dies without an imam because he has failed to obey his amir, he will die the barbaric death of a an infidel.”

(From Ahmad)

Twenty-Eighth Hadith

The Prophet (PBUH) spake thus:

"He who draws back from his Amir and goes onto die, on the day of judgement, to save him from the torment of this crime, there will be no argument on his behalf and he who separates from the congregation and then dies will die the barbaric death of an infidel."

(From Ahmad, Muslim, Al-Hakim, Al-Tabrani)

Twenty-Ninth Hadith

The Prophet (PBUH) spake thus:

"The Imam is the Blessing of God on earth. He who honours God's sultan will find on the day of judgement that God honours him. And he who insults God's sultan, God will disgrace him on the day of judgement."

(From Al-Tialasi)

Thirtieth Hadith

The Prophet (PBUH) spake thus:

"Those people around the sultan who have the intention that they will disgrace him, before the day of judgement god will disgrace them."

(From Al-Hashemi)

Thirty-First Hadith

The Prophet (PBUH) spake thus:

"Respect the sultan who comes after me, he who wishes disgrace on the Sultan (or Amir) and ceases obedience to them, he has made a great breach in the bastion of Islam, even the repentance of such a person will not be accepted until he resumes his obedience."
(From Ibn Asim)

Thirty-Second Hadith

Hazrat ibn-e-Omar relates that he was sitting with some of his companions when the Prophet turned towards them and said:

"Do you people not know that God sent me to you as his prophet?"

The reply was, "yes, indeed, we give witness that you are undoubtedly the prophet of god."

The Prophet (PBUH) spake thus:

Do you not know that he who obeys me definitely obeys God, and this too that obedience to me is obedience to God.

They replied

"Yes indeed, we give witness that he who obeys you truly obeys god and give witness to this too, that obedience to you is truly obedience to god."

The Prophet (PBUH) spake thus:

"Truly it is the command of God that you obey me. And my command is that you obey your Ameers. And I say it again – Obey your Ameers."

(From Abu Ali)

Thirty-Third Hadith

Hazrat Arfjah RATA states that then he heard The Prophet say:

"After me there will be sudden disasters or misfortunes, as some person will leave the congregation, or another will try to cause splits and differences in the community of Mohammad, even when they are united and in agreement. Kill such a person, whoever he is. Pay no attention to his family or his status or his personality in this matter also pay no attention to Satanic menaces or religious issues, for the help of God is surely with the congregation and Satan lies in wait for those who protect the congregation in order to give them trouble."

(From Muslim Abu Daoud, Ibn Asim, Ahmad, Abdul Razaq, Al-Tabrani)

Thirty-Fourth Hadith

The Prophet (PBUH) spake thus:

"Anyone who dies in a state without having the responsibility of Obedience to an Amir, he will die the barbaric death of an infidel, and he who, after giving allegiance, then takes off and casts aside his obedience, on the day of judgement he will find that god ignores him and leaves him without respite."

(From Ahmad, Abu Ali, bn Asim, Hashemi)

Thirty-Fifth Hadith

The Prophet (PBUH) spake thus:

"He who shows me obedience he has truly shown obedience to god.
And he who disobeys me has truly disobeyed god. And he who obeys the Amir has definitely truly (or undoubtedly) obeyed me. and he who disobeys the amir has definitely disobeyed me. The Amir is the Shield."
(From Muslim)

Thirty-Sixth Hadith

The Prophet (PBUH) spake thus:

"Without a doubt, the Imam is a shield, under whose protection rescue is achieved."
(From Bukhari, Abu Daoud)

Thirty-Seventh Hadith

The Prophet (PBUH) spake thus:

"Anyone who causes division within my community, behead him, whoever he may be."
(From Ibn Asim)

Thirty-Eighth Hadith

"It is not justified to shed the blood of a Muslim who has declared his faith in the prophet and oneness of god, but if he fulfils one of these three conditions – adultery with a married woman, murder or forsaking his religion and leaving the congregation."
(From Bukhari)

Thirty-Ninth Hadith

The Prophet (PBUH) spake thus:

“Whoever disobeys his amir and leaves his congregation, he will die the barbaric death of an infidel. And who fights only for prejudice, nation or tribe will also die the barbaric death of an infidel.”

Fortieth Hadith

The Prophet (PBUH) spake thus:

“The merit of one day of action of the righteous Imam is more blessed than sixty years of worship. To deliver even one divine punishment to the corrupt offers more goodness and blessing than the rain of forty days.”

(From Al-Tibrani)

Section Three

AVOIDING LUST FOR PROPERTY AND OFFICE

All mujahideen must keep their hearts pure from the lust for property and office or else they will face humiliation in this world and eternity

God instructed said or spake thus:

"The ultimate End will be good for those people who have no desire to exalt themselves in the earth nor to make mischief and the good end is for those who guard against evil" (Qur'an 28:83).[16]

The Prophet (PBUH) spake thus:

"You will covet the Emirate although this will be a source of shame on the day of judgement."
(From Bukhari, Al-Nisani, Ahmad)

The Prophet (PBUH) spake thus:

"O Abd-ur-Rahman! servant of Merciful God, do not desire the Emirate or office. For if you receive office without having asked for it you will have god's help. But if you receive an official position having demanded it you will not have god's help but in fact you will be handed over to the office.

From him who has desired a post for himself and obtained it through lobbying, it will be taken away. But in the case of he who takes up a post having been obliged to do so, god will send down an angel to keep him on the right path."

(From Bukhari, Muslim, Tirmizi, Abu Daoud, Ahmad)

The explanation of the above is that every individual should properly take stock of himself and look deep into his heart to check that in some corner of that heart lurks not some desire for position and office.

Section Four

NO OFFICE IS GIVEN TO THE ONE WHO DESIRES IT

The amir is obliged to refrain from appointing anyone to a position or office who desires such. If those who desire office are appointed then it will sully and do great damage to the aims of the movement and will represent a betrayal of the task which has been entrusted to the Amir.

The Prophet (PBUH) spake thus:

"By God, we will never confer office on someone who himself demands or desires that office."
(From Bukhari, Muslim)

Section Five

THE ACTIONS THROUGH WHICH OFFICE BEARERS CAN STAY ON THE RIGHT PATH

It is the duty of the Amir to maintain close monitoring of all position holders and office bearers under his Emirate, and such principles should be formulated for them, by which, instead of desire for position and office, they can instead be filled with love of God. Instead of the desire for women, the spirit of doing jihad and fighting against the enemy on the battlefield should increase daily. You should be impatient for the highest office of martyrdom and the risking your life, like a fish out of water.

In this connection I would point out a few important issues:

From time to time, office holders, specially those office-based gentlemen to whom resources are entrusted, and those working in sensitive departments, must be sent to the front-line. No important worker or comrade/friend must be held back from the front. When they witness the danger of war, when the observe the martyred and the wounded, when they spend a few moments in a hail of bullets, then surely they will learn about death and the afterlife and will repent their sins and seek forgiveness. From the blessings of the battle-field their spirit of martyrdom will be increased. In addition, they will appreciate the requirements and difficulties of the military fronts and the challenges of the mujahideen.

This will develop in them sympathy, patience, thankfulness and restraint. The blessing of these qualities will imbue their service to Shariat, according to the Shariat, with light and spirituality.

POSTS AND RESPONSIBILITIES SHOULD BE ROTATED WITHIN AN APPROPRIATE DURATION

No one should stay in a post so long as to become synonymous with that office, that they start to think that the post cannot exist without them, that they are indispensable. In this regard the process of changes and transfers within the Taliban Movement ordered by the Amir ul-Mu'mineen is very positive. God willing it will be extremely fruitful in the long run.

DO NOT MAKE ANY POST SO ATTRACTIVE THAT OTHER PEOPLE WILL DESIRE IT LUXURY

It should be ensured that no post or office provides such opportunity for and enjoyment that others start to desire it and grab for it.

WHY IS THERE SUCH A LACK OF BLESSING IN MOST RELIGIOUS MOVEMENTS NOWADAYS?

Nowadays, in religious movements normally, official positions are made so attractive that people are prepared to do anything to capture the office. Separate groups and factions are formed and different campaigns conducted and in order to reach this official position the asserters of Islam engage in such snatch and grab and are involved in such actions that would embarrass an animal. As result many large movements which were on the brink of success, simply perish. If opportunities for luxury and enjoyment are removed from official positions offices and the sense of responsibility and hard work can be made into its defining feature. This will keep away differences and animosities and then at the time of being transferred the office holder will not find it too difficult.

ENSURING THAT PEOPLE ARE DILIGENT IN VOLUNTARY PRAYER, RECITING AND CHANTING GOD'S NAME

In general people who stay far from the battle field show little diligence in voluntary worship. Therefore it is necessary to ensure that all post holders and people working in offices should be made to be diligent in their worship, especially voluntary prayers, reciting and reciting god's name.

A principal cause of weakness in religious movements is their lack of bonding with God. For bonding with God, it is necessary to be regular both in compulsory religious duties as well as voluntary worship.

Section Six

THE IMPORTANCE OF ADVICE

In the Koran and the hadiths every amir is instructed that, for important matters he should seek the advice of his companions who have three qualities

1. Virtuous and sincere
2. Well loved
3. Experienced

To understand the importance of advice it should be suffice to note that the prophet ordered:

“Take counsel with those companions” (Qur’an 3:159).[17]

The prophet received direct instructions from god and who could have better sense and understanding than the prophet. Nevertheless the order to see advice is given so that the amirs should understand the importance of advice.

And he said:

“And they approached every task by taking advice among themselves”. (Qur’an 42:38).[18]

The Prophet (PBUH) spake thus:

“No one was successful based upon his own opinion and no one failed after taking advice”.

When the prophet made Muaz bin Jabal the judge of Yemen and dispatched him, he instructed:

“Take advice because those who take advice receive help from Allah. Advice is taken from those who are trustworthy.”
(From Bukhari)

The Prophet (PBUH) spake thus:

“There can be no failure after looking for the omens and there can be no shame after taking advice”.
(From Al Jami Al Hadith)

Hazrat abu Huraira says:

“I have never seen anyone on a par with the prophet in the abundance of advice that he took.”
(From Al Mansoor)

Hazrat Hassan says:

“Whichever tribe seeks advice from amongst themselves, they will definitely be pointed in the right direction.”
(From Sultani)

Hazrat bin Abbas stated:

“When the ayat vashavar rehem fi ul amar was revealed, the prophet said,
Be aware, that God and his prophet had no need of advice. But God made this decision as a blessing on my community, so that whosoever amongst teh community will seek advice, they will not find the right way difficult to access.

And whosoever dispenses with this, they will find that the wrong road is not difficult to access."

(from Ibn Adi, Al-Behaqi)

The Amir ul-Mu'mineen, Hazrat Omar stated:

"Take advice from god-fearing people"

(From Al Baqwi)

Section Seven

AFTER TAKING ADVICE THE AUTHORITY TO DECIDE RESTS SOLELY WITH THE AMIR

Just as Shariat has commanded the Amir to take advice, Shariat has also given the amir full authority to select the shura and to make the final decisions.

SELECTION OF THE SHURA

It is best that at the time of the selection of members of the shura there should be consultation with virtuous, well-liked, experienced friends. In the case of difference the amir's opinion will be the authority.

2. Apart from this the amir is authorised to appoint a permanent Shura or temporary Shura. Then when he considers it suitable, he may also change the permanent status of the Shura into a temporary one, He may add people to it or remove people from it, or bring about changes and improvements in the shura.

3. The shariat also gives the amir the permission, despite the existence of a permanent or temporary shura, to seek the advice of anyone who is qualified to give advice, and is not a formal member of the shura.

4. The amir also has the authority to form a separate shura for each department or to form a general shura spanning all departments.

THE STATUS OF THE SHURA IN THE SHARIAT AND THE RULES GOVERNING THE METHOD OF CONSULTATIONS

Remember well that the purpose of ordering consultation with the shura or advisers was never to impose the decision of the shura as binding on the amir or to force the amir to accept the advice. After the ayat "Vashavar rehem fil amar" (giving a role to the shura), God said, at the time of making a decision, trust in god. In Shariat, the status of the shura is simply to advise, ensure that all the different aspects of an issue, should be brought to the attention of the amir, Members of the shura in giving advice, should do so with complete integrity and remember the instruction of the prophet:

The adviser is holy

It is incumbent on the advisor that he must avoid breaching any trust, he should give sound advice and when he leaves must avoid leaking any secret.

When the shura has given its advice, it has finished its work. Instead of interfering in the work of the amir they should pray that god should provide the amir with such inspiration that he may make a beneficial decision.

6. When should the shura meetings take place and who all should be invited? On this issue too the amir can be given advice but the final decision is his.

7. The amir should keep the number of shura members down. If there are too many shura members then at times this can cause problems, in fact very serious problems. If the shura has too many members then this can cause dissent.

Section Eight

SPECIFIC GUIDANCE TO THE MEMBERS OF THE SHURA

DIFFERENCE OF OPINION

A differences of opinion is not a bad thing, it is natural and bound to occur. Hazrat Musa and Hazrat Haroon had many differences of opinion, as did the prophet and his companions. Hazrat Sheikheen had a difference of opinion about apostates and Zakat. In this same way there are plenty of other such instances, not all individuals have the same level of sense and understanding.

This proves that differences of opinion are inevitable. If there arises a difference of opinion between the shura and the amir; because the whole of our movement is dedicated to the supremacy and practical enforcement of shariat, therefore on such an occasion we should determine what is dictated by shariat and apply it to ourselves, otherwise he who is unable to apply shariat to the six feet of his body, how will he be able to enforce the rule of God on the world?

God instructed:

“If some dispute arises in deciding on a matter refer that matter to god and his prophet” (Qur’an 4:59).[19]

If differences arise in some matter, then for a decision turn to god (Qur’an 42:10).[20]

THE SHARIAT POSITION ON DIFFERENCES IN OPINION BETWEEN THE SHURA AND THE AMIR

The quotations from the Koran and the hadith show that the prophet and the caliphs instructed, as well as the opinions of theologians and the collective decision of the community affirmed that in the case of difference of opinion between the shura and the amir, it is as clear as day, and well-established for all the Muslim community that only the amir's decision will be final, for if not that the amir will become an employee and the employee an amir and the whole of our system will be destroyed.

THE AMIR'S COMMAND IS THE COMMAND OF SHARIAT AND THE AMIR'S DECISION IS THE DECISION OF SHARIAT

When the amir makes a decision which goes against the opinion of the advisor or shura then it is obligatory that the shura accept wholeheartedly and have no resentment or dissatisfaction in their hearts. They should not be upset in their hearts.

Testament number two included the ayats and hadith which give the order for obedience to the amir and demonstrate that obedience to the amir is obedience to god and the prophet and disobedience to the amir is disobedience to god and the prophet.

When the amir makes a decision against the opinion of the shura, because this decision has been declared to have the status of Shariat, therefore no one is to make any move against it, nor voice their opinion against it, since this would be going against Shariat, which, once the decision is taken, is not dependent on any further evidence.

TRUST IN THE BENEFIT AND BLESSING OF THE AMIR'S DECISION

Because the amir's decision has the force of shariat trust that in it lies benefit and blessing, however unsuitable it might seem, do not advocate the rightness of your your opinion, even if it is apparently one hundred percent right.

5. If some harm results from the implementation of the amir's decision, consider that this is good that your opinion was not followed as in that case even more damage would have been done.

If the amir takes the advice of an adviser then that adviser should not go outside and claim that this was my advice. Other than dissatisfaction amongst the community, there are many disadvantages of this, from which problems can arise for the adviser also.

If a member of the shura or any other office bearer defies the shariat guidance and orders regarding obedience to the amir, then he should prepare himself to face all those warning given in the koran and shariat against opposing the amir. Such a person will be counted as disobedient to the amir and a traitor too to the shariat.

On such an occasion I call upon all mujahideen, especially members of the shura and office holders, to study the quotations and hadith given in section two.

THE METHOD FOR GIVING ADVICE TO THE AMIR

Members of the shura or other ordinary mujahids should continue to give the Amir good advice, it is necessary that they speak in an appropriate and respectful way. The Shariat gives guidelines on how to give advice to the amir.

“Whoever wants to give advice to the amir should not do so in public (thereby humiliating him) but should respectfully take his hand and advise him in privacy. If he agrees then praise be to god and if not then at least the counsellor has done his duty.”

Notes

1. This anecdote and the details of Rasheed's education and career are taken from an autobiographic note he included in his published collection of fatwas. Ahmad, Mufti Rasheed, "The best decrees (ahsan al fatava)" (Urdu), Islamic Affairs Publishers, New Delhi, 2012.
2. The Rasheed Trust is listed as a sanctioned entity by the U.N.committee operating under Security Council Resolution 1267, http://www.un.org/sc/committees/1267/1267.pdf (accessed 9/915). The listing states "Involved in the financing of Al-Qaida and the Taliban". The South Asia Terrorism Portal provides additional details of the case against Rasheed Trust http://www.satp.org/satporgtp/countries/pakistan/terroristoutfits/Al-Rashid_Trust.htm (accessed 9/9/2015).
3. The South Asia Terrorism Portal: http://www.satp.org/satporgtp/countries/pakistan/terroristoutfits/Al-Rashid_Trust.htm
4. The author represented the Office of the UN Coordinator in these negotiations.
5. The listing is available from http://www.un.org/sc/committees/1267/1267.pdf
6. The role of *Eta't Amir* as a guide to Taliban internal doctrine and organisational culture is further explored in Semple (2015), available at http://www.usip.org/publications/rhetoric-ideology-and-organizational-structure-of-the-taliban-movement

7. 42:13 — “The same religion has He established for you as that which He enjoined on Noah – the which We have sent by inspiration to thee – and that which We enjoined on Abraham, Moses, and Jesus: Namely, that ye should remain steadfast in religion, and make no divisions therein: to those who worship other things than Allah, hard is the (way) to which thou callest them. Allah chooses to Himself those whom He pleases, and guides to Himself those who turn (to Him)”.
8. All translation from the Qur’an are taken from: “The Holy Qur-an : text, translation & commentary” by Abdullah Yusuf Ali (Lahore: M. Ashraf, 1938).
9. 8:46 — “And obey Allah and His Messenger. and fall into no disputes, lest ye lose heart and your power depart; and be patient and persevering: For Allah is with those who patiently persevere”.
10. Rasheed cites references for all his hadith. Many references are to multiple collections, as in this hadith, for which he cites to collections of Muslim, Bukhari and Ahmad. For most hadith he gives a volume and page number, or a simple page number. The hadith collections include multiple variations of some hadith, based on different original narrators. Rasheed reflects this by citing and distinguishing the variations. All this makes for intricate and elaborate references, which are in many cases longer than the text of the hadith which Rasheed quotes. Below we have condensed Rasheed’s referencing by simply footnoting the principal collections which he cites.
11. 3:103 — “And hold fast, all together, by the rope which Allah (stretches out for you), and be not divided among yourselves; and remember with gratitude Allah.s favour on you; for ye were enemies and He joined your hearts in love, so that by His Grace, ye became brethren; and ye were on the brink of the pit of Fire, and He saved you from it. Thus doth Allah make His Signs clear to you: That ye may be guided”.

12. 3:105 — “Be not like those who are divided amongst themselves and fall into disputations after receiving Clear Signs: For them is a dreadful penalty”. 3:106 — “On the Day when some faces will be (lit up with) white, and some faces will be (in the gloom of) black: To those whose faces will be black, (will be said): “Did ye reject Faith after accepting it? Taste then the penalty for rejecting Faith.””
13. 30:31 — “Turn ye back in repentance to Him, and fear Him: establish regular prayers, and be not ye among those who join gods with Allah”, - 30:32 — “Those who split up their Religion, and become (mere) Sects, – each party rejoicing in that which is with itself!”
14. 61:4 — “Truly Allah loves those who fight in His Cause in battle array, as if they were a solid cemented structure”.
15. 4:59 — “O ye who believe! Obey Allah, and obey the Messenger, and those charged with authority among you. If ye differ in anything among yourselves, refer it to Allah and His Messenger, if ye do believe in Allah and the Last Day: That is best, and most suitable for final determination”.
16. 28:83 — “That Home of the Hereafter We shall give to those who intend not high-handedness or mischief on earth: and the end is (best) for the righteous”.
17. 3:159 — “It is part of the Mercy of Allah that thou dost deal gently with them Wert thou severe or harsh-hearted, they would have broken away from about thee: so pass over (Their faults), and ask for ((Allah)’s) forgiveness for them; and consult them in affairs (of moment). Then, when thou hast Taken a decision put thy trust in Allah. For Allah loves those who put their trust (in Him)”. Rasheed cites the ayat by number but only gives a highly condensed version of the text.

18. 42:38 — “Those who hearken to their Lord, and establish regular Prayer; who (conduct) their affairs by mutual Consultation; who spend out of what We bestow on them for Sustenance”. Again Rasheed gives a condensed version.
19. 4:59 — “O ye who believe! Obey Allah, and obey the Messenger, and those charged with authority among you. If ye differ in anything among yourselves, refer it to Allah and His Messenger, if ye do believe in Allah and the Last Day: That is best, and most suitable for final determination.” Rasheed gives a condensed version.
20. 42:10 — “Whatever it be wherein ye differ, the decision thereof is with Allah. such is Allah my Lord: In Him I trust, and to Him I turn.”

About the Editors

Michael Semple is currently Visiting Professor at the Institute for Study of Conflict Transformation, Queen's University, Belfast and a Director of conflict-focused NGO, Talk for Peace. Michael has practised and written on humanitarian assistance and conflict resolution. During the period 1988 to 2008 he worked in Pakistan and Afghanistan for international NGOs, the United Nations and the European Union. He was a member of the United Nations political team which helped implement the 2001 Bonn Accords and as Deputy to the European Union Special Representative for Afghanistan 2004-08 participated in the follow-up to those accords. Throughout his career Michael has sought to be a reflective practitioner. Since 2008 he has worked as a scholar and adviser on conflict transformation, with particular focus on the Afghan conflict. He has directly advised key policy makers concerning the conflict in Afghanistan, particularly with regards to political engagement with the Taliban. Michael has researched and published extensively on Islamist militant movements, with a focus on the Afghan Taliban.

Yameema Mitha is a writer and editor on social issues. She has worked as a journalist during the turbulent Zia years in Pakistan, as country representative for Oxfam in Pakistan, and as Principal of Mazmon-i-Shauq, a unique bilingual school in Pakistan, committed to developing an indigenous system of education fostering peace in South Asia, and she maintains a strong interest in education.

She has written on women in the informal labour force in Pakistan, on women and Islamic law in Pakistan, and on religious minorities in Pakistan. She has an abiding interest in the classical arts of the Indian subcontinent, specially music, has lectured on Indian cinema, acted in theatre in both Pakistan and Ireland, and lives between the two countries.

Other Books Published by First Draft Publishing

I am Akbar Agha: Memories of the Afghan Jihad and the Taliban
Sayyed Mohammad Akbar Agha

Following in the tradition of Mullah Zaeef's My Life With the Taliban, Akbar Agha's memoir tells a story of war, friendship and political intrigue. Starting in 1980s Kandahar, the difficulties and successes of the mujahedeen come through clearly as Akbar Agha struggles to administer a group of fighters. He details the different groups fighting in Kandahar, their cooperation and the scale of the Soviet Union's efforts to crush them. Not directly a participant in the Taliban government that ruled post-1994, Akbar Agha offers a sometimes-critical account of the administration built by many of his former fighters. After the fall of the

Islamic Emirate in 2001, Akbar Agha was involved in the Jaish ul-Muslimeen opposition group and for the first time he has revealed his account of what happened in the kidnapping of UN aid workers. I Am Akbar Agha ends with an analysis of the problems afflicting Afghanistan and outlines a vision for the political future of the country post-elections and post-2015. Anand Gopal has written an introduction to the book.

"Mandatory reading"

— Graeme Smith, Senior Analyst for Afghanistan

Kandahar Assassins: Stories from the Afghan-Soviet War
Mohammad Tahir Aziz Gumnam

Assassinations are a near-daily occurrence in Afghanistan. Whether by rogue Afghan security forces or by lone individuals roaming the cities and districts, the threat of a target killing is very real. Kandahar Assassins offers an unparalleled view of this phenomenon from the perspective of the assassins. Published in 1986 in Pashto and a perennial classic in Kandahar's bookstores, Kandahar Assassins tells the story of two well-known assassins who operated in the southern city during the 1980s war. The stories of 'Lame Ghazi' and Commander Ghaffari involve ambitious raids and plots carried out within the Afghan-controlled city. This book offers a corrective to the idea that assassination is a new phenomenon in Afghanistan. Mohammad Tahir Aziz Gumnam was a doctor working in Pakistan at the time, allowing him access to a variety of figures within the Afghan mujahedeen. Originally from Kandahar, Gumnam offers insight as an Afghan who was close to both the events and the people he describes. Judging from this book, the style and manner of assassinations in southern Afghanistan doesn't appear to have changed much. Kandahar Assassins, therefore, offers a unique perspective on the world of these target killers and how they carry out their operations. It is an essential read for any soldier serving in Afghanistan as well as those seeking to understand the history behind the current conflict. Dr David Kilcullen wrote the introduction to this English translation of the book.

"a Thousand-and-One Nights of the Afghan jihad... a detailed and lyrical account of the war that he and his contemporaries fought against in Kandahar during the 1980s"

— Dr David Kilcullen (from his introduction), counterinsurgency expert and author

An Undesirable Element: An Afghan Memoir
Dr Sharif Fayez

This is the incredible story of a relentless educator named Sharif Fayez, born in 1946 in Herat, Afghanistan, who bore witness to the Communist invasion of 1979, the Iranian revolution of 1979, and who authored a ground breaking PhD dissertation that forever linked the best American poetry to Afghanistan by proving that Walt Whitman had read and been inspired by Rumi. It is the story of how Sharif pursues education above all else and becomes a professor at Kabul University only to flee illegally to Iran when the Soviets invade, where he becomes caught in the violent Islamic revolution as a professor at Mashad University. Surviving the Afghan and Iranian governments' ruthless campaign to silence academics and their students, as well as the Iran-Iraq War, he becomes a prominent voice of resistance against the Taliban and extremism in the 1990s, writing hundreds of articles, and ultimately returns to Afghanistan as a signatory to the 2001 Bonn Conference and as the Minister of Higher Education. He completely overhauls the Afghan education system, restores co-education to the country and establishes six new universities. He is almost single-handedly responsible for the incredible strides the Afghan education system has made since 2002.

"An Undesirable Element is a fascinating tour through the tumultuous years that helped create modern Afghanistan. Fayez survived Soviet Afghanistan and revolutionary Iran, only to find himself watching from exile as his country devoured itself. Improbably, he returns after 2001 to help resurrect Afghanistan's devastated higher education system, giving an insider account of the challenges of building education in a land dominated by warlords and fundamentalism. The result is a poignant reminder of how much Afghanistan has endured, and the flicker of hope that remains despite it all."

— Anand Gopal, author of *No Good Men Among The Living*

"A compelling read, An Undesirable Element recounts an Afghanistan many have forgotten. It serves as a rallying cry to once again imagine all that country might be. It's a tale as extraordinary as the land from which it comes."

— Elliot Ackerman, author of *Green On Blue*

"An Undesirable Element moves fast as flames and offers a luminous account of the last half century of Afghan conflicts and redevelopment. Trevithick's oral history of Sharif Fayez's story is a trove: from a kiss on the head by the Afghan former King Zahir Shah, Fayez's life intersected with the future leaders and quiet supporters of his country—both heroic and tyrannical—from Columbia University to a Post-revolutionary University in Mashad, Iran. Fayez is a modest but robust storyteller whose eventual position as Afghanistan's first Minister of Education after the Taliban is only one of the strange twists and turns his story offers. His deft handling in the rebuilding of Afghanistan should be read by anyone interested in how one can use patience and determination to bring hope to a country reduced to rubble."

— Adam Klein, editor, *The Gifts of The State: New Afghan Writing*

"The term visionary tends to be misapplied to those who are merely headstrong. But it is a perfectly apt description for Sharif Fayez, the most important figure in education in 21st-century Afghanistan, yet one that history may have neglected without his memoir. Such an omission would have deprived future generations of Afghans from understanding how Fayez, perhaps more than any single person, created hope for the country's young minds at the turn of the millennium and, in so doing, altered a nation's destiny."

— Martin Kuz, Freelance journalist

Milton Keynes UK
Ingram Content Group UK Ltd.
UKHW020655281123
433408UK00014B/1479

9 783944 214214